Contents

Body parts

Our bodies have many parts.

head

skin

arm

foot

leg

Our bodies have parts on the outside.

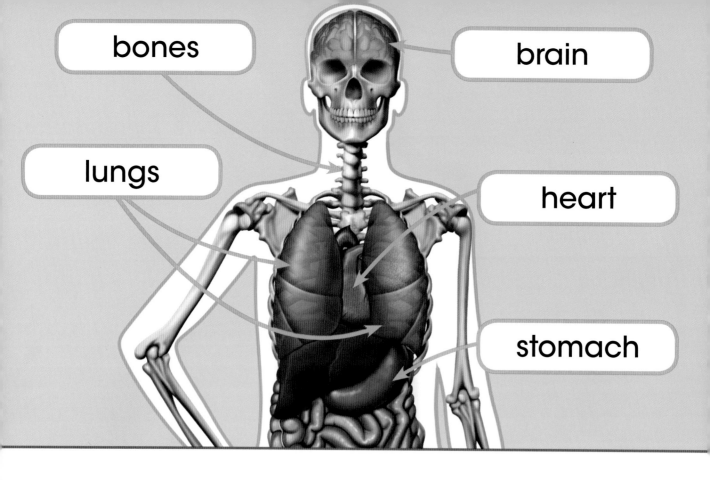

bones

brain

lungs

heart

stomach

Our bodies have parts on
the inside.

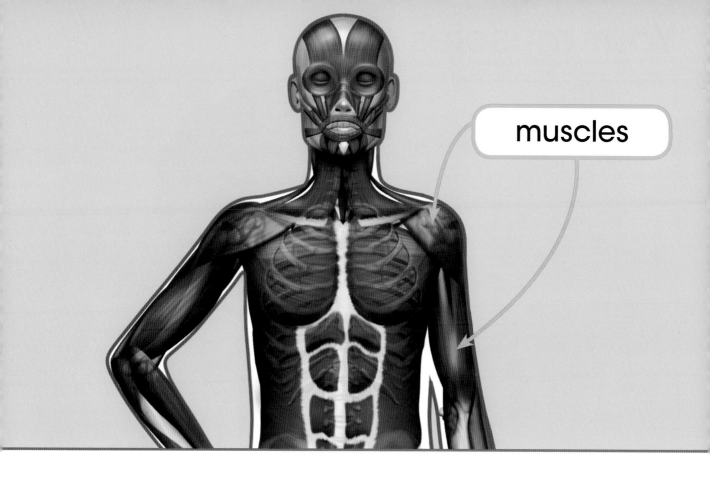

muscles

Your muscles are inside your body.

Your muscles

You cannot see most of
your muscles.

Your muscles are all over your body.

You can feel your muscles.

muscle

You can see the shape of
some muscles.

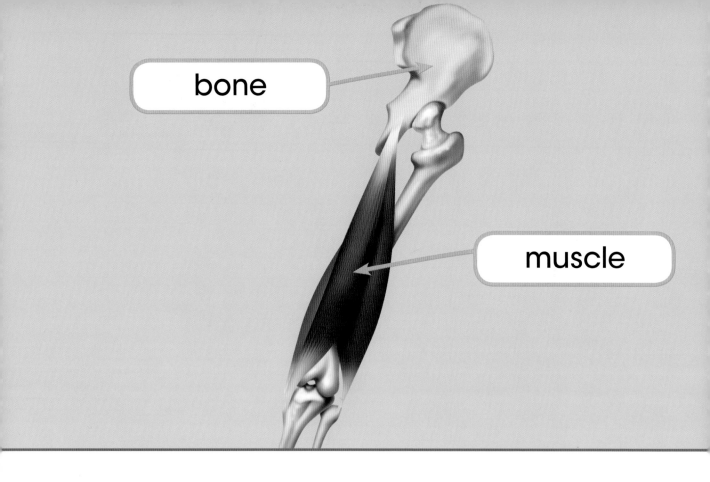

bone

muscle

Some muscles are joined to
your bones.

The muscles pull on your bones to make them move.

What do muscles do?

Your muscles make your
body move.

You can choose to move
some muscles.

Some muscles help you
move about.

Some muscles help you smile.

Some muscles work all the time.

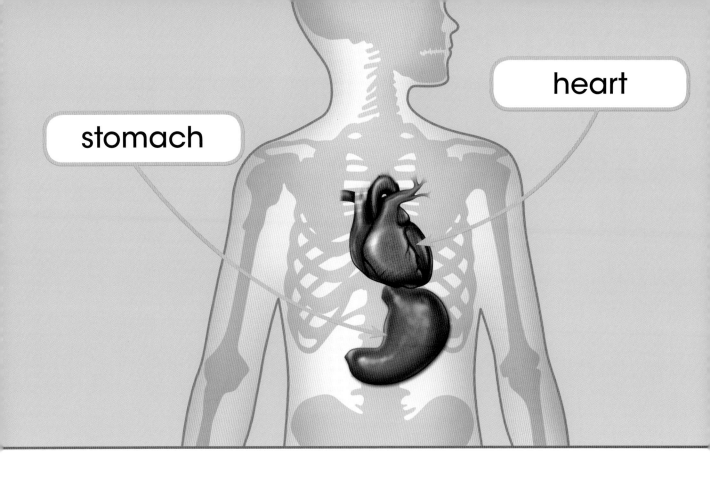

stomach

heart

Your heart and stomach muscles
work all the time.

Staying healthy

You can exercise to help
your muscles.

You can eat healthy food to help your muscles.

Quiz

Where in your body are
your muscles?

Answer on page 24

Picture glossary

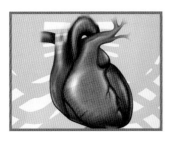 **heart** a muscle inside your chest. Your heart beats all the time so that it can push blood around your body.

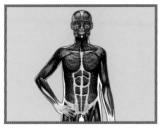 **muscles** stretchy parts inside your body. Some muscles help you to move your body.

 **stomach** a muscle inside your tummy. Your stomach breaks food into tiny bits so that your body can use it.

Index

Answer to quiz on page 22:
Your muscles are inside your body.

Notes to parents and teachers

Before reading

Ask the children to name the parts of their body they can see on the outside. Then ask them what parts of their body are inside. Make a list of them together and see if the children know what each body part does, for example, food goes into their stomachs. Discuss where their muscles are and see if anyone knows what our muscles are for.

After reading

- Ask the children to step up and down or do jumping jacks for a minute (timed by you). When they have stopped, ask how their legs feel. Discuss how exercise can make our muscles ache and the importance of not straining our muscles.
- Put the children into pairs and ask them to count how many times the other child blinks in a minute (timed by you). Compare the answers and then explain how a muscle in our eyes makes us blink without thinking. Discuss why we need this muscle to work like this.